Jim Arnosky

FROZEN WILD

HOW ANIMALS SURVIVE
IN THE COLDEST
PLACES ON EARTH

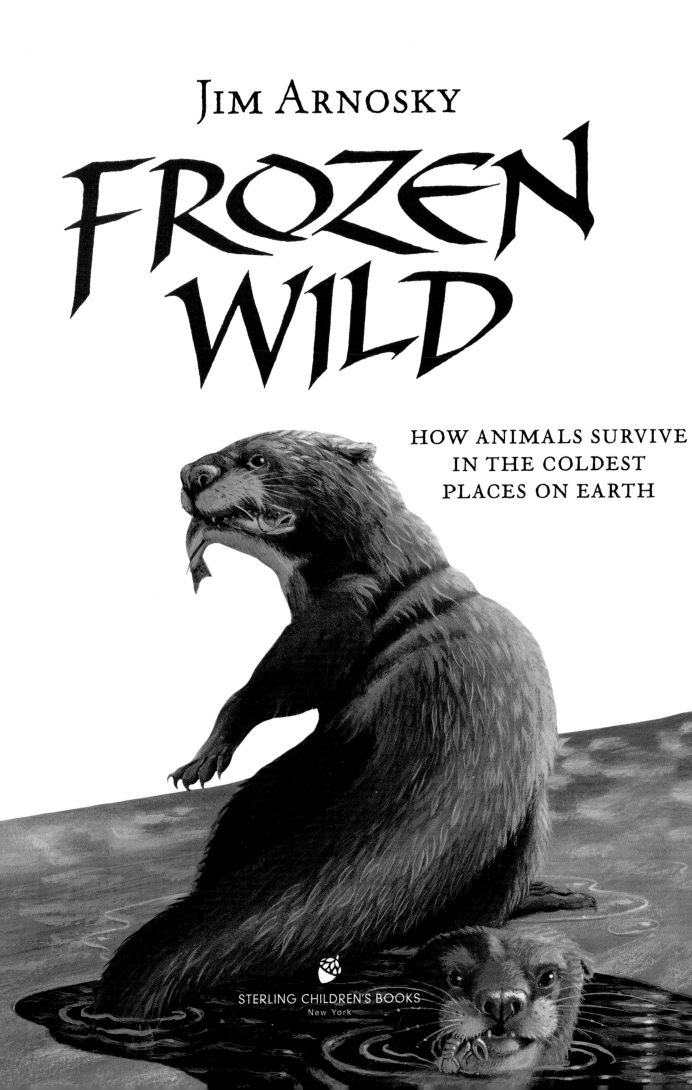

STERLING CHILDREN'S BOOKS
New York

FOR SIERRA

STERLING CHILDREN'S BOOKS
New York

An Imprint of Sterling Publishing
1166 Avenue of the Americas
New York, NY 10036

The artwork for this book was created using pencil and acrylic paints.
Display lettering created by Paul Shaw.
Designed by Philip Buchanan.

ISBN 978-1-4549-1025-1

Distributed in Canada by Sterling Publishing
℅ Canadian Manda Group, 664 Annette Street
Toronto, Ontario, Canada M6S 2C8
Distributed in the United Kingdom by GMC Distribution Services
Castle Place, 166 High Street, Lewes, East Sussex, England BN7 1XU

For information about custom editions, special sales, and premium and
corporate purchases, please contact Sterling Special Sales at 800-805-5489
or specialsales@sterlingpublishing.com.

Manufactured in China
Lot #:
2 4 6 8 10 9 7 5 3 1
6/15

www.sterlingpublishing.com/kids

CONTENTS

CROWS

Introduction

Quietly it comes. The first frost coats the plants and footpaths. Then ice encases small streams and ponds. Snow falls. Big lakes freeze over. Mighty rivers flow more slowly, turning to slush. And the north wind blows. Winter is here and even in the coldest regions of our planet, every living thing must adjust somehow to survive.

Our seasons are caused by the strange fact that, unlike the other planets in our solar system that spin upright, Earth is tilted $23\frac{1}{2}$ degrees on its axis. Because of this tilt, different portions of the Earth's surface are exposed more directly to the sun's rays at different times during the year-long trip. Northern winter occurs when the North Pole is tilted away from the sun. Winter in the Southern Hemisphere happens when the North Pole is tilted toward the sun. As I write this, the North Pole is tilted away from the sun and winter has a vise-like grip on the North Country where I live. But I am warm inside my house, with a hot fire crackling in the woodstove.

This book is about the wild animals of snow-covered fields and forests, the great northern plains, vast stretches of frozen tundra, and icy polar regions—wild animals that have to survive day after day, night after night, out in the cold. I've been outdoors every day walking in their tracks, learning more about their lives in winter. Dress warmly and follow my snowshoe trail. Let's learn together.

Jim Arnosky

5

RIVER OTTERS

Under the Ice

When a landscape is frozen and covered with snow, water still flows and fish still swim under the ice that forms on the rivers and lakes. It is cold down deep, but not freezing. River otters find openings in the ice to dive through and hunt for fish and crayfish. Otters hunt in a circuit of "plunge holes" that takes about two weeks to complete. Every fourteen or fifteen days, the otters in our area of Vermont show up on the frozen pond near our barn. They break away any thin ice that has formed on their plunge hole and dive in.

The fish and crayfish, sluggish in the cold water, are easy prey. Every few minutes an otter pops to the surface with something it has caught and climbs up onto the ice to eat. On windless days, even from afar, I can hear them chomping their food. I get to watch them for a couple of days before they go on to the next frozen pond and plunge hole in their hunting circuit.

Semi-aquatic animals such as otters, mink, and mergansers have webbed toes for swimming. They also have oily fur or feathers that are waterproof to keep the skin beneath dry and warmly insulated, even when swimming underwater.

Mergansers and other diving ducks stay in wintry places as long as there is some open water to dive into. When these places ice over, the birds fly southward.

Otter tracks showing webbed toes.

Mink are too small and light to break even thin ice. They search for natural openings in river ice to dive through.

Mergansers can swim under the ice in less than a foot of water.

9

When the air is very cold, you can actually see the beavers' body heat escaping through the lodge peak, like smoke rising from a chimney.

Muskrats make small "houses" of aquatic plants. In winter, they forage under the ice for plants. When food becomes scarce, muskrats eat the inside walls of their house.

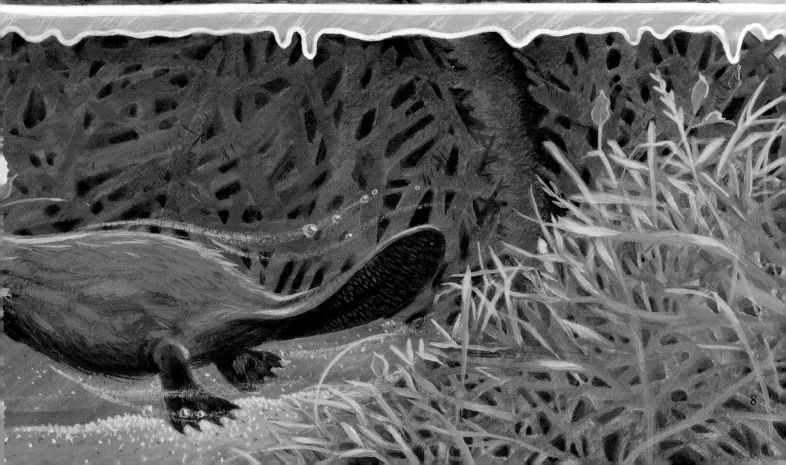

BEAVERS IN WINTER

Beavers build a lodge by piling thick branches and heavy logs on the pond bottom. The buoyant wood is anchored down with mud. While the beavers work, they feed on leaves, bark, and the moist nutritious layer of wood just under the bark. Once the mound is piled four or five feet above the water surface, the beavers swim down to the base of the mound and chew a tunnel up through the wet wood to the dry wood above the water level. There, they chew an inner chamber in which to live.

After the entrance tunnel and inner chamber are completed, the beavers plaster the outside of the lodge with mud, sealing in all but the peak, which allows air to flow through. Inside, the beavers' body heat warms the chamber.

A beaver lodge is an impenetrable fortress that even the largest predators cannot claw into.

A beaver can swim under the ice back and forth from the lodge to the food pile in complete safety.

MOOSE AND SNOWSHOE HARE

Snow Travelers

One big factor in an animal's survival outdoors in winter is how well it can get around in snow to find available food and also run to escape danger. Small, lightweight animals such as squirrels and mice run on snow without sinking deeply into it, or they can tunnel through it to get from feeding spot to feeding spot. Foxes, bobcats, and lynx grow extra hair around their feet, creating natural snowshoes. And, as their name suggests, snowshoe hares have very large hind feet that keep them on top of the snow.

Deer, however, are especially vulnerable in deep snow. Their slender legs and sharply pointed hooves poke deep narrow holes, bogging down the deer and making it difficult—if not impossible—for them to run from predators. In snow country, deer "yard up" under the sheltering boughs of evergreen trees. There, the deer tramp down a maze of trails in the deep snow so they can run from danger and move about as they feed on evergreen buds.

The largest member of the deer family, the moose, has little trouble getting around in deep snow. A moose's enormous hooves punch wide holes in snow and its powerful leg muscles pull each step out quickly enough to be able to run if need be.

In the Arctic, polar bears travel by running on the frozen ocean. When the ice begins to melt and break apart, the bears swim from one floating ice pack to another.

Porcupines travel the same routes daily, creating gully trails packed down by their flat oval feet.

The deeper an animal's body sinks into snow, the harder it is to travel fast or far.

White-tailed Deer

Red Fox

Moose

Snowshoe Hare

3 feet of snow

ARCTIC ANIMALS

Animals that live in the Arctic year-round roam the frigid landscape and swim in Arctic waters searching for food. Warm-blooded mammals and birds must eat constantly to keep warm. Fish feed whenever they can, and as *much* as they can to maintain their strength for swimming against the cold, powerful water currents.

The narwhal is an Arctic species with a long, spiraled tusk. The tusk is one of two front teeth that, in male narwhals, grows through the skin and keeps growing. A narwhal uses its pointed tusk to fight other male narwhals during breeding season.

The harbor seal is named for its habit of frequenting harbors and shipping ports.

The beluga is a small Arctic whale that feeds on fish. It is the only all-white whale.

The polar bear feeds primarily on seals but will eat anything it can get its claws into. A polar bear is so strong, it can even dive into the water and kill a small whale such as the beluga.

Walruses and seals are slow and clumsy on land but graceful and swift in the water.

A walrus's tusks are not used for eating. They are for fighting other walruses.

KILLER WHALES

The Arctic

At the northernmost portion of the globe is the Arctic Ocean, with the North Pole in its frozen center. The area known as the Arctic Circle includes the Arctic Ocean and many islands and parts of the continental United States, Canada, Greenland, Scandinavia, and Russia.

Within the Arctic Circle are vast areas of ocean, ice pack, glaciers, mountains, rivers, forests, and treeless plains called tundra. Such diversity of habitats supports a variety of wild animals.

During the long northern winter, so much of the Arctic is tilted away from the sun that the temperatures can drop to -80 degrees Fahrenheit. In such extreme cold, it takes a thick layer of fat and a very dense coat to keep an animal from freezing solid. Arctic mammals such as polar bears, seals, walruses, and whales—all of which swim in the frigid water to get from place to place or to catch their food—have either waterproof fur or an extra thick layer of fat called blubber to keep them warm.

A thick skin plus 3 inches of blubber keep a walrus insulated from the arctic cold.

There is no actual pole in the ice at the North Pole, of course. The North Pole is just a measurement of the exact point marking the northernmost point of planet Earth.

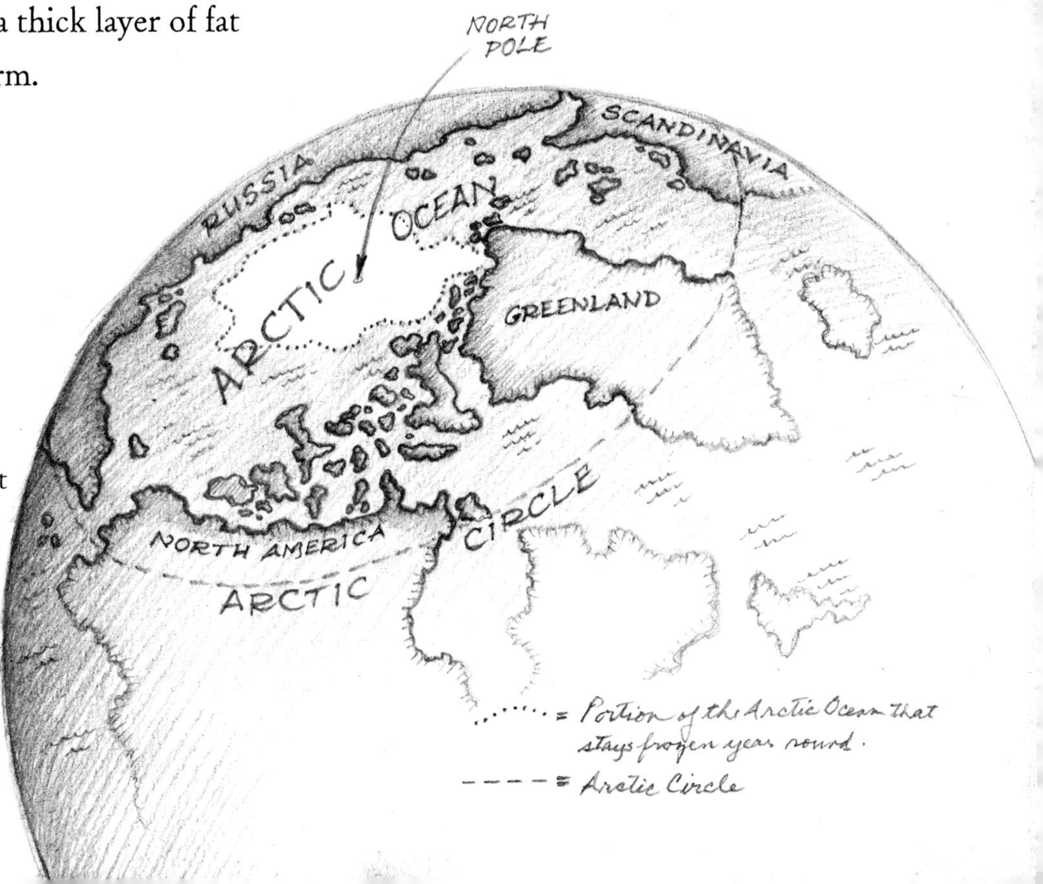

NORTH POLE

RUSSIA
SCANDINAVIA
ARCTIC OCEAN
GREENLAND
NORTH AMERICA
ARCTIC CIRCLE

Killer whales, shown at left, frequent Arctic waters, hunting together for seals, dolphins, belugas (small white whales), and even swimming bears.

.... = Portion of the Arctic Ocean that stays frozen year round.

- - - - - = Arctic Circle

16

The snowy owl can be found in the Arctic year-round. But when food becomes scarce, snowy owls fly south into Canada. Some snowy owls winter in the United States.

The gregarious Arctic hare lives in groups of 10 to 100 or more. During snowstorms, they crowd together to keep each other warm. When danger threatens, they disperse and run every which way, confusing predators.

Musk oxen live in small herds on the Arctic tundra. In winter, they dig down in the snow as deep as three feet in order to feed on the vegetation beneath.

Arctic grayling live in clear, cold freshwater streams and lakes.

Lake trout are freshwater fish that inhabit only deep, cold lakes.

Arctic foxes are brown in summer and white in winter. They live on the tundra and rocky Arctic coasts.

Ptarmigans are chicken-like birds that are white in the winter and brown in the summer. They live in the Arctic year-round.

The musk oxen's main predator is the Arctic wolf. When confronted by wolves, a herd of oxen face the danger together, forming a circle, all heads and horns facing outward, with the most vulnerable among them in the center.

Over 240 species of fish swim in the Arctic Ocean, with the cods being among the most numerous. (Shown above is the Atlantic cod.) Flounder, skates, rays, and some species of sharks also live in the Arctic.

The wolf of the Arctic is the timber or gray wolf. Gray wolves can be gray, brown, black, or pure white in color.

RED FOX

Staying Warm

You wouldn't go outdoors in the cold without wearing a winter coat. Wild animals live outdoors all the time, and in winter, those that do not migrate to warmer places grow winter coats to keep them warm. A mammal's winter protection is made up of three parts: an extra layer of fat under the skin, a woolly layer of dense fur, and a sleek, water-shedding outer coat of guard hairs.

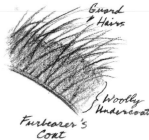

chickadees with feathers fluffed.

Furry animals such as foxes, beavers, weasels, wildcats, and wolves all have a dense woolly undercoat that traps body heat and holds it, and an outer coat of luxurious guard hairs. An animal's coat covers completely, so no spot on the animal's body is unprotected. When you see an animal with snow piling up on its back, that's a sign that no body heat is escaping and the animal is warm.

Birds are protected from winter wind and cold by a layer of soft, fluffy down that is covered by the birds' feathers. In extremely cold weather, a bird can raise and fluff its feathers so the air trapped beneath them, heated by the bird's body, adds another layer of warmth. In fact, many animals, including humans, have tiny muscles in the skin that lift hairs in reaction to cold air. That's what goose bumps are all about!

Deer change from a summer coat of fine, glossy hairs to a winter coat of longer, thicker hairs that are hollow and have air trapped inside them for added warmth.

Deer Hair (Summer)

Deer Hair (Winter)

Guard Hairs

Woolly Undercoat

Furbearer's Coat

Some animals, such as the Arctic fox and the snowshoe hare, have the extraordinary ability to change color from summer brown to winter white to camouflage them against the snow. The color change happens gradually.

October   *November*   *December*

Penguins are large, hardy, flightless birds with feathers so dense they look more like fur. A penguin's thick, oily coat of feathers keeps the bird warm in sub-zero temperatures on land, and dry in the frigid ocean, where penguins swim to feed on fish and squid.

Over 200 species of seabirds fly to Antarctica every summer to breed in huge colonies. Almost all live in the Southern Hemisphere. The Arctic tern flies all the way from the Arctic in the Northern Hemisphere.

On land, penguins hobble around walking upright, or they slide on their bellies. In water, penguins are sw and agile and can dive de to find fish.

MACARONI PENGUIN
Height: 28 inches

CHINSTRAP PENGUIN
Height: 30 inches

ADELIE PENGUIN
Height: 28 inches

The largest Antarctic seal is the leopard seal, which is ten feet long and weighs 1,000 pounds. This big aquatic predator feeds on fish and penguins.

LEOPARD SEAL
Length: 10 feet

ANTARCTIC ANIMALS

The always frozen continent of Antarctica is mostly uninhabited. There are no terrestrial hunters prowling like the bears, wolves, and white foxes found in the Arctic. No snowy white owls swooping. There are only penguins, seabirds, and seals. These summer visitors congregate on the narrow band of ice-free shoreline and on floating ice sheets.

Emperor penguins stay in Antarctica year-round.

Gentoo Penguin
Height: 32 inches

Young penguins are round and plump and do not go in the water until they are large and strong enough to escape leopard seals, sharks, and killer whales.

King Penguin
Height: 35 inches

Emperor Penguin with Young
Height: 42 inches

The only mammals on Antarctica are seals. Every summer a number of seal species breed on the rocky shore. The smallest of these is the Antarctic fur seal. It grows to be five feet in length.

Antarctic Fur Seal
Length: 5 feet

ARCTIC TERNS AND ADELIE PENGUINS

...rctica

...is composed primarily of ocean. At
...ite end of the globe is Antarctica, the fifth
...ntinent in the world. It is a desolate place. Most
...rctica's terrain is covered year-round by ice many
...nds of feet thick, making it the coldest place on Earth.
...eratures as low as -135.8 degrees Fahrenheit have been
...ded near the South Pole.

...n winter, so much of the surrounding ocean water freezes
...r that it doubles the surface area of the continent. In
...mmer, when the ocean ice melts, so does some of the coastal
...ce. Penguins and shorebirds come to nest amid the rocks and
...sand, and seals congregate to breed.

The oceans that surround Antarctica are rich with life, from
microscopic plankton, tiny shrimp-like Antarctic krill and fish,
to the great blue whale, the largest of Earth's creatures. A blue
whale consumes thousands of pounds of krill a day, and grows
to be 100 feet long, weighing one ton per foot.

ATLANTIC OCEAN

INDIAN OCEAN

ANTARCTIC CIRCLE

ANTARCTICA

PACIFIC OCEAN

SOUTH POLE

....Extent of winter ice

Antarctic Krill (actual size)

Blue Whale

SOUTH POLAR SKUA
Wingspan: 3½ feet

The albatross's tubular nostrils
are not outwardly evident.

WANDERING ALBATROSS
Wingspan: 9½ feet

Because there are no large predators or
small animal prey on the ice-covered
continent, Antarctica's surrounding ocean
is the hunting and feeding grounds for
mammals and birds alike.

(All penguins shown here are painted in
size proportion, with the emperor penguin
being the tallest at forty-two inches.)

The wandering albatross,
three feet tall with a wingspan
of almost ten feet, is the
largest seabird in the world.

The emperor penguin is the greatest of all diving
birds, capable of diving 2,000 feet deep!

The most numerous Antarctic birds are the skuas, petrels, and albatrosses. Petrels and albatrosses are members of the "tubenose" family. These birds all have extra large, tubular nostrils that greatly enhance their ability to locate food (fish or fish scraps left behind by boats) by smell.

SOUTHERN GIANT PETREL
Wingspan: 7½ feet

TUBULAR NOSTRILS OF A PETREL

guins migrate seasonally by water. Their
flipper-like wings propel them along. They
e to Antarctica from other places in the
thern Hemisphere. There are
enguins in the Northern
nisphere.

ANTARCTIC TERN

ARCTIC TERN
Arctic and Antarctic terns are almost identical except for the Arctic tern's overall grayer color. Terns are surface feeders that hover over water seeking small fish and crustaceans.

GREAT HORNED OWL

Wild Perfection

Some clear winter night, sit by the window inside your warm house and stare out at the starlit world. Think of all the wild animals living out in the cold—birds with their feathers fluffed against the chill and mammals cloaked in fur, curled on snowy beds. In your own bed, curl as they do and try to imagine having your body be the only source of heat to keep you warm.

Sometimes I feel sorry for animals in the frozen wild and sometimes I am envious of them. I envy their physical perfection that makes them able to live their entire lives outdoors in the purity of fresh, open air—cleansed by rain and snow, strengthened by wind, warmed by the sun during the day and their own inner fire at night. I live in awe of wild things.

Author's Note

I began this book in winter and found inspiration for the paintings of snow-country wildlife in the snowy fields and woods around our Vermont farm. By the time I had begun the Arctic section of the book, my wife, Deanna, and I had migrated south to a warmer climate, and I worked into the springtime creating paintings of whales and seals, polar bears and penguins in their icy polar habitats. I thought it would be difficult to paint cold country scenes without the snow and ice outside my window, but it wasn't. I had plenty of excellent reference books, photos Deanna had taken of polar animals in zoos, and snapshots of seals and seabirds I had taken in the North Sea, when I was a young U.S. sailor stationed in Europe.

You don't have to travel all the way to the Arctic to see some of the Arctic animals depicted in this book. A number of species of whales and seals that spend part of the year in the Arctic Circle are the same species that we see offshore along the Atlantic and Pacific coasts at other times of the year.

Many species of birds that breed in the Far North migrate south in the winter. And others, like the snowy owl, which is a year-round Arctic animal, will fly south in winter to find better hunting grounds. Every winter someone spots a snowy owl in the United States. And each and every year, Arctic terns fly from the Arctic Circle to Antarctica and back, stopping off at various beaches to rest. Their marathon annual migration makes them the long-distance champs of all migrating birds, flying as many as 25,000 miles round trip! Whenever you use a bird guide to identify a bird you are seeing, check its range to see where it might be found at different times of the year. You will be surprised to discover how far some travel.

Read all you can about wildlife in winter. Keep track of the seasonal migrations of birds. Start a list of all the birds you see and find out which of them leave your area to fly south in the winter and which have flown all the way from polar regions to spend the winter where you live. Pay attention to what impacts wild animals globally and can even threaten their survival—important issues such as air and water pollution, habitat-destroying weather events, climate change, and global warming. As crazy as it may seem, the coldest, harshest, most inhospitable places on Earth need to remain as cold and frozen as they can be in order to preserve the ice that polar animals walk on, and prevent rocky shorelines where seabirds and seals breed from flooding over.

From pole to pole, our beautiful blue planet is an oasis of life spinning slightly tilted through space. And it is that tilt creating our seasons that has fostered a diversity of interconnected living things that we are only beginning to truly understand. It is my hope that, in reading this book, you understand winter and life in the coldest regions of the globe a little better and have gained a greater appreciation for the frozen wild.

More about Animals in Winter

Arnosky, Jim. *Crinkleroot's Guide to Giving Back to Nature.* New York, NY: Penguin Putnam Books for Young Readers, 2012.

Brandenburg, Jim. *Face to Face with Wolves (Face to Face with Animals).* Washington, D.C.: National Geographic Children's Books, 2010.

Cowcher, Helen. *Antarctica.* New York, NY: Macmillan Publishers, 2009.

Holland, Mary. *The Beavers' Busy Year.* Mt. Pleasant, SC: Sylvan Dell Publishing, 2014.

Lynch, Wayne. *Penguins!* Richmond Hill, ON: Firefly Books LTD., 1999.

Matthews, Downs. *Arctic Foxes.* New York, NY: Simon & Schuster Children's Publishing, 1995.

Miller, Sara Swan. *Walruses of the Arctic (Brrr! Polar Animals).* The Rosen Publishing Group, New York, NY, 2009.

National Wildlife Federation website, "Global Warming;" nwf.org/globalwarming.

Papastavrou, Vassili. *DK Eyewitness Books: Whale.* New York, NY: Dorling Kindersley Limited, 2004.

Rosing, Norbert. *Face to Face with Polar Bears (Face to Face with Animals).* Washington, D.C.: National Geographic Children's Books, 2009.

Schulz, Florian. *To the Arctic.* Seattle, WA: Mountaineers Books, 2011.

Simon, Seymour. *Global Warming.* New York, NY: HarperCollins Publishers, 2013.

Simon, Seymour. *Penguins.* New York, NY: HarperCollins Publishers, 2009.

Taylor, Barbara. *DK Eyewitness Books: Arctic and Antarctic.* New York, NY: Dorling Kindersley Limited, 2012.

Tulloch, Coral. *Antarctica: The Heart of the World.* Brooklyn, NY: Enchanted Lion Books, 2006.

United States Environmental Protection Agency website, "Climate Change;" epa.gov/climatechange.

October   November   December

Other Books in this Series

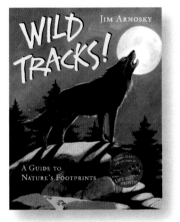

WILD TRACKS!
A Guide to Nature's
Footprints

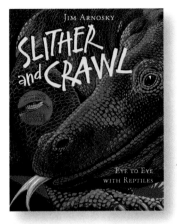

SLITHER AND CRAWL
Eye to Eye with Reptiles

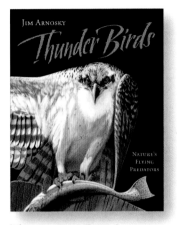

THUNDER BIRDS
Nature's Flying Predators

CREEP AND FLUTTER
The Secret World of Insects
and Spiders

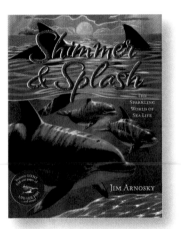

SHIMMER & SPLASH
The Sparkling World
of Sea Life

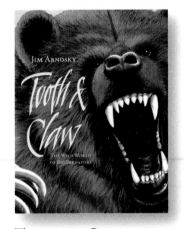

TOOTH & CLAW
The Wild World of
Big Predators

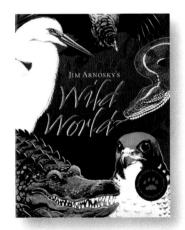

JIM ARNOSKY'S
WILD WORLD